7 REASONS WHY YOU ARE HEADED TO A FINANCIAL CRISIS AND DON'T EVEN KNOW IT
BY
ERNST BAUDIN

Copyright © 2019 by Ernst Baudin

This book is designed for informational purposes only and is not meant to take the place of advice from a qualified financial planner or other professional. The author of this book disclaims liability for any losses that may be sustained as a result of applying the methods suggested in this book.

All rights reserved. No part of this book may be reproduced or used in any manner without written permission of the copyright owner except for the use of quotations in a book review. For more information, address:
coachingwithernst@gmail.com

FIRST EDITION

www.masteryourpersonalfinance.com

CONTENTS

Intro..1
First Story 12
Second Story..18
Third Story 26
Fourth Story 35
Fifth story..43
Sixth Story 52
Seventh story 62
Then there was the end 73

INTRO

This book was written for you, yes you, the one who will take the time to read it. It was written for people who want more out of life, for people who think "there has to be a better way. There has to be something that can be done. There must be something. I know this way of life cannot be all there is." This book is for you if you are inclined to think this way. If you want more out of life than stuff, but want real freedom to do what you want and when you want it then this is a good place to start.

I will not give you answers, or do the work for you; we all have different paths and different interests in life. We are, in essence, different beings with different goals and dreams. What I am willing to do is to help you see a common ground that we all have, that is often missed or totally discounted. One area almost everyone who lives on this planet is subject to yet do not think is important and can go on doing what they see others do. ?

We were taught how to spend, and we are always reminded what is the best product on the market and what new product will be coming soon. We are taught that money is too complex and we need to give it to someone else to be handled for us. We are taught that we need the latest of this and the latest of that. Before, we would only replace items when they no longer worked, but now we live in a consumer-based society and having us consume is the way things work now. We need to consume for this economy to get back in shape. One thing is left out though, and what is left out is what affects us the most.

When all you do is consume and pay bills, the companies are growing bigger and they will hire more people and yes, there might be more jobs. That is good for everyone else, but there are no real strong messages reminding us we need to take care of ourselves. Not just buying things we feel we deserve because we worked hard but having a way to not be affected when things take a down turn. When you spend all you have, who will be there for you when you need it? Whom will you tell? There a needs for balance, you cannot consume or spend 100% of what you have.

One thing we are not taught is that our income is the most powerful tool we have to build wealth. When we see how some individuals and companies make millions or even billions by selling something to customers, we can see that our income is a powerful tool. But no one taught us how to use that tool for our wealth and not just for someone else's wealth. There is nothing wrong with spending, but do it while also keeping some of it for you, and your family, when you need it most.

We see all those families in need and people needing the basic things, but no one really being there to help them. Yet people are there when they are doing well and have money to spend. When times are tough, that is when you see where your actions can lead you. When times are tough, we do not care about the latest items and things we used to want. Our focus changed from consumerism to what is really important. That's different for all of us, but basic needs, like food and shelter, things we normally take for granted, now becomes our primary focus.

Wouldn't it be nice to have those covered, regardless of what happens in the economy? Even if there is a local and global economy, we all have our own personal economy, and that is the one that affects us the most and the fastest. We are in control of that economy, and how we behave in it, will show how we handle the tough times. Because when things are good does not show you how well you are doing. Your plans and actions are really tested during tough times, that is when you will know if you have been doing things that can only lead to hard times.

Just like it is easy to be happy when it is a beautiful sunny day, the same thing goes for when we have money to spend, our basic needs are covered, and we have extra money to travel and indulge in every single one of our needs. It is then we say money does not matter, what we say does not matter and is not a big deal is often something we have covered. If you have food and shelter, they will not matter much to you, but if for some reason you lose your home and have no idea where you will sleep, and have no one to really take you in, or you feel that is too much to ask. That is when you will understand how important those basic needs are.

When we have a lot of money and extra to spend on other things, worrying about food and shelter are not even existent for us, they are just a given. What is a given is only a given for as long as you can afford it, and for the ones living paycheck to paycheck, you are a few paychecks away from being in trouble. It is like dreaming, and one day you wake up look around and noticed you have nothing left but a bunch of items you can't do much with, items that will not feed you, or pay the rent or mortgage.

You might try to sell some items, but how fast can you sell them, and how much can you make? Can you make enough to cover your income for even two weeks? How long can you keep selling items to cover all your basic expenses? Chances are, not long enough, because we do not know how long it will last and we have no idea when it is coming. We only expect good times and for the most part only live in the moment without paying a thought for tomorrow. Some of us have been taught to pay no thought for tomorrow because tomorrow will take care of itself.

This is all good, but some of us also have been taught to prepare for a rainy day. Yes, you have to prepare for a rainy day. The same way it is never always 100% sunny, is the same way it will rain in our lives. If you do not have an umbrella and no shelter, and it is pouring rain, you will wonder how come you didn't buy an umbrella when you had the money, and even worse, how come you did not think of having enough to keep your life the way it is, regardless of what happens. You will look at people with umbrellas and people with shelters and remember the good times.

The good times do not have to go, and they can stay if during the good times you are able to see and prepare for those rainy days. When you are prepared, you can enjoy watching the rain from your home and it can be an interesting day. Lack of preparations shows itself when you are tested. The problem is that it is a pop quiz, and we do not know what the questions will be, but we can study. And we study, by preparing ourselves. The ones who are not prepared are the ones who will suffer the most and the problem is, no one really painted a picture of where or what will happen if you do not get ready for a rainy day.

That picture must be painted with so much doom and gloom that it wakes those of us that have been in deep sleep forever. We tend to follow what is marketed to us and those are often, in simple terms, "we have what you need, and your life will be better with this, to get it, just send us your money" once you get the item, you use it a few times and toss it away until the next time you see a new shiny object. It is the same way when we were kids and wanted a toy, the moment we got it, we played with it a few times and then we were done.

It was no longer something new; the appeal of new is soon gone with familiarity. Then we seek something else, and you guessed it, that new item will become familiar in no time and we will back browsing for something else to buy. If that is all we do with our money, there is no way we can be ready if anything happens, we will wake up and wonder where it all went and we only wonder when we need it the most. We miss what we had only when it is gone, but when we have it, rarely do we see its value and how much we really had.

The saying "you do not know what you have until it is gone" is true for many of us. If we could see what we have, when we have it and use that insight to take care of it, we will enjoy it without regret and make it last longer. What we get to keep is our memories and how much we lived. But we will lose those fast if there is nothing left and we are in survival mode. Survival mode has no desires other than staying alive and that is not a place we can be happy in.

What we have now, and what we are enjoying might be where we want to be or it might not be. But we are in control of where we are headed to some extent, based on our level of preparation. You can never be too prepared, but you can be underprepared. Having an overflow will allow you to share and be there for others who have less. When you have less you will be in need of someone else's generosity, you get to choose where you will be based on your level of preparation. The more you have set aside, the more you will be prepared regardless of what goes on in the economy in general.

When you are well prepared it does not matter what happens, you will last longer than anyone that is not prepared at all. You are the government of your own economy, you are the only president, and no one can take your power away. But you can be seduced by clever emotional based marketing that will entice you to spend your money, marketing that does not have your best interests at heart. When you do this often enough you will be deeply in debt, you will not be able to cover all that debt, and you will be in debt for years.

You can create your micro economy; in fact we all do, but never took the time to realize it. We often complain and think why is the government or the people in power, always spending and over spending while most of us are overspending ourselves. Not only do we overspend, but we also take out loans at much higher interest rates than the government does. We have to remember, people in a position of power come from society, and society as a whole, spends more than they make, and are deeply in debt. Those people represent what is most common in society today.

It is so easy to judge, while most of us cannot even manage our own micro economy, in which we have a few to no people to take care of. We have less to do and it is much simpler and easier, yet many of us are in trouble. You would assume, with less income and less responsibility we would be able to have great success with our personal finances, but in general, we do not. There is more and more debt and less and less savings. Your ability to save and be in control will be the determining factor of your financial journey.

We learn by modeling, we do what we see and what we are taught. The problem with this is if we are not taught how to properly manage money, and all our closest examples are doing something a certain way (like getting into debt) we will just do what they are doing, without really questioning it. Without really seeing who it really benefits, and how we will suffer the consequences. We just do because we see others do. And we are advertised what to do, without thinking that those advertisers and companies have their best interest in mind, not ours.

The money you have can make a change in your life, or in someone else's, you get to choose, and you choose with what you do with it. Every time money is spent, wealth is created and wealth is depleted. We can see this easily with math and the banking system. Let's say you buy something for $100 and do not even think about it, because for you that is not a big ticket item. What happens is that money is taken out of your account; this is where the minus comes in. Then that amount is deposited in someone else bank account; that is where the plus comes in.

This might be simple, but do not miss it. You are now $100 poorer and the company that sold you the item is $100 richer. The more you do this, the poorer you will be, and the richer everyone else you give your money to will be. We also need to understand that companies are in business to make a profit, but what they sold you for $100 is not worth $100, otherwise they would not be in business for long because they need to make a profit. It is worth $100 to the customer, but it cost them less to make it. They are becoming richer and the speed depends on their profit margins.

There is nothing wrong with making a profit and getting richer, but we also need to keep some of that money and build our own wealth. Because so far, what we see and are advertised the most, is to build someone else's wealth. Showing support to a company that has a great product and that you place value on is perfectly fine. However, you also need to remember your financial interests. Yes, you incorporated, meaning you are your own economy. If your economy is based 100% on spending, even on good products, you will go broke and will be out in the street when it rains.

You need to remember that your main job is to build your economy, then support the rest of the economy by buying what you believe in. If there is no you, there is no support of anyone else. You will be more of a burden on the economy when you need support; so supporting yourself is an important part of helping your local economy. If we considered our lives as business and at the end of each year we would sit down and see how well we have done, we would drastically change our behavior and focus more on building our micro-economy, so we do not put pressure on the local economy because we are not prepared and are in need of assistance.

We live our lives without looking at the numbers, knowing what is happening and where we are going. We just spend, enjoy ourselves and do not sit down for a second to see what we have left after years of working, or even decades, depending on how old you are. Memories are not just trips and items we purchased they can also be in the form of savings. It would be nice to have something left from a job you worked years or decades ago. Why is it normal that we can work for years and have nothing left as if we had never worked a day in our lives?

As I am writing this, I can say I have worked for at least 15 years, but do not have much of that income from those 15 years of employment, and have no idea where it went. How can we spend our working lives enjoying items without having anything left when we need it the most? One day I looked at my finances and wondered how come I have nothing left? How come I did not think of saving a certain percentage? A percentage that would be there for years and never to be spent, but saved? How come it is all gone and all the items that I bought with that money are gone as well? We are left with nothing basically because items have a short lifespan.

If all our money is used for cars, clothes, electronics etc. We will not see what happens. The reason is that we will not keep those items long enough and we will constantly change them. Getting rid of the old and replacing with the new, and after doing this for a while nothing is left. It becomes like a revolving door that we are always in, without taking time to come out and look at it for what it is. One day we wake up and wonder what happened and wonder how come no one told us about this, for some people it was too late, they lived their lives and have now passed on. For the rest of us, there is still time.

If you sit down and think of what you have been doing with your money and have no clue where it went chances are you will be wondering the same thing later on. If we told our money what to do we would not wonder where it went because we would know where it went and where some of it is still is. When we have no plans we can't look back and ask questions, because answers are found when creating a plan. If you do not have a plan, it will be hard to see what happened. If you plan to spend so much on a particular item, you will know how much you spend on that item. If you just spend you will have to investigate afterward and to do so, you will need to find clues.

Our financial lives should not be looking back and finding clues and wondering what happened. We have a bad association with the word budget, we think it will be limiting and would stop us from enjoying life. The obvious thing that is missed is that we forget that we are the ones that will be making that budget or financial road map. This is when premeditation is a good thing. When you plan for what is to come you will not be looking for clues. A financial road map will show you where you are going and you can look back and see where you have been. Being lost and asking for directions and not remembered the roads you took, is where most of us end up.

If you want to end up somewhere, plan for it and look at the roads you will take that will lead you there. All the financial roads lead to savings, because if you have no savings, you will not be going anywhere fast. You will sit there wondering how come you cannot travel. The best thing that can happen to anyone is to understand that the income they are making today is their biggest tool to build wealth. They get to choose for who it will be used, themselves or someone else.

Before you can get on the road and change your financial life you have things inside yourself that you need to let go of that have been limiting you. We all have stories, and ways to see things or believe how things are, that are affecting us without us even knowing it. Without removing those, you will not be able to get started and your chances of success are limited, as you can see from your track record. We have all been there, until we read a book, thought about it differently or got some help.

My goal in this book is to show you some of those weeds in your garden that are stopping you from blossoming. I have divided those into seven stories most of us have about success and money that are stopping us from achieving what we say we want to achieve. I am doing this in order to help you save some time and be the best you can be, and also because I wish someone would have written something like this for me to stumble upon. I know it would have changed things for me and my life would be different. I am paying it forward to anyone who wants more out of life.

This is written to make you think and get started on your journey. This is not the only thing you need to read, and reading will not be enough, you will need to take action. Because nothing changes until you do and you act. One thing you can do, is share this book with people you know, not for me, but for you, because change is a lot easier when we are doing it as a group and with like-minded people. You might have friends or family that are wondering the same things about their finances but never really mentioned it to you, the same way you may not have mentioned it to them. Increase your chances of success by involving others in the beginning of your financial journey.

This what not written for me, and it is not for everyone. It is only for people who are ready to make some changes. If you are ready and you share it with someone else, you will know if they are ready to make some changes too. It will be a good way for you to know without sharing too much and a nice way to avoid negativity from others that might affect you from even getting started. Having others to support you and who feel the same way will be easier, because you will find ways together to reach your goals faster.

You have to read this with an open mind and not for anyone else because this is for you. What you think and the way you see the world will only affect you and the people close to you. I am not asking you to agree with me or disagree with me, but to take those ideas, bounce them around in your head and see if they could be beneficial if you applied them in your life and the potential direction your life would take if you acted on them. Action will change your life; agreeing or disagreeing will leave you where you are.

FIRST STORY

Job security is an illusion, a story we tell ourselves because we are scared of how things are. Our job is linked with a lot of factors out of our control. All those factors make our jobs not secure. No one in a company has 100% warranty that the company will last forever. You can have all the good intentions and have good employees and care about them, but no one can stay in business or keep their jobs if their business is built on something that can become obsolete.

When I was a kid we used to go out, choose a movie, rent it and come home and watch that movie. If the movie we wanted to see was rented and there were no extra copies we had to choose something else. If you worked at a blockbuster or any movie rental service, regardless of how good an employee you were, your job is already gone. Now if I want to see a movie I don't need to go out and it is always available for me to see.

I remember when I was younger, how my mom would go to a travel agent to book her flight to Haiti, our home country. How she would make payments and have the agent book the flight for her. As you know things have changed and her travel agent was replaced by a website. Most middleman businesses are replaced by websites. You might have been a good travel agent, studied for it and even had your own company, but when technology changes you are out of a job. You will be phased out by convenience and cheaper prices.

Before, if you wanted to write a book you needed to find a publisher and that publisher needed to believe in you. Now anyone can write anything and self-publish it, and keep all the income. With online publishing and websites like Amazon anyone can be an author, share their ideas without the need to find a company that will believe in them and publish their books. You can be global and your book can be bought around the world and there is no profit sharing with a middleman.

You do not control your job security, not even your boss, or the owner of the company does. Because when technology replaces an entire industry, everyone is out of a job. Everything that can be consumed in a digital format has made the transition or is about to make the transition. Even at the grocery stores, someone noticed they were paying people to scan items, accept money, and give back change. The next thing they did, replaced the cashier with a self-checkout register.

The thing with our society we think about ourselves first. If no one was using them or wanted to use them it would have failed, but since most of us want what is best for us, we will go use the self-checkout machines. We do not want to wait on anyone or have to potentially deal with someone with a bad attitude, or who simply do not like their job. So we go use the self-checkout register.

The truth is we will do what is best for us, what will save us time and what will keep our life simple. We will book online, we will join Netflix, download movies, stream videos online. We will read articles online, and buy books online.
Everything can be done from the comfort of our homes or our mobile without mobile devices. We do not participate directly in all the industries that took jobs away. When it came to robots in factories maybe, but for other industries, we agreed and moved on with the times.

You might not believe or see how your job can be in jeopardy now. It is normal, not being able to foresee technology. All those jobs and few industries I listed here are just a few examples of people losing it all. There is much more coming we can't even imagine. Simply said, no one has job security but last one to lose their job, is the owner. If you are not the owner, you will lose your job before he/she does. If he/she has no job security, you do not either.

We have all seen big companies cutting hundreds if not thousands of jobs at once. All those employees believed they had job security. The thing to remember here, those events are always unexpected. Not expecting it, is important in this equation. Since we do not know what new technology will come and replace and change our lives we have to be prepared. How do you prepare for the unexpected?

There is an expression that goes "do not have all your eggs in one basket". If you have all your eggs in one basket and you drop the basket, you have nothing left. If you have all your life based on your paycheck coming in every two weeks. If you have nothing left and you are waiting for the next paycheck so you can continue living, you are a paycheck away from problems. We see it coming; yet do not do anything about it. We believe in magic, nothing will change, it will get better, just because.

I am sorry to tell you, the only way things go when we do nothing, is down. If you do not work out, you will be out of shape. If you eat only junk food, you will gain weight. If you go to bed late, you will be tired. If you are living paycheck to paycheck you will end up losing it all. When we let go, things only go down the drain. The natural inclination is for things to get worst. If you spend all your money, how can you have anything left?

If you want to be in shape, you have to work out. If you want to be healthy and slim, you have to eat the proper food. If you want to be rested, you have to get enough sleep. If you want to avoid financial trouble, you need a safety net, a sleep well at night account. Anything worth something will require some effort. If you are not willing to make the effort, you and the people you are responsible for will be the ones suffering. Thinking things will always be the same, is the kind of thinking that cause people to lose it all.

You can create a job loss simulation. If you have no money coming in for one month, what would your life look like? What will you do? Where will you end up? How long can you live with zero money coming in? Will your rent or mortgage be late? What other bills will not be taken care of? You can answer those questions and see what can happen. If you are able to get unemployment, what will you do during the wait? Unemployment is only a fraction of your income, how long will that sustain you?

Some of you might be thinking of using credit during that time. The problem with using credit when we are in financial trouble is that sooner or later, we will have to make payments for the amount we took. Yes, those payments might be small in the beginning but without knowing how long you will be in trouble, taking more and more money will only make that payment something you cannot pay back. Using credit during an emergency is only adding an extra payment for you to pay while you have no money coming in. What will you do? Use the money you took from the card to pay the card?

When you are in trouble financially due to a loss of income, the last thing you want is an extra bill. That is considering that your card had no balance before the job loss. If your card already had a balance, you are just digging a bigger financial hole while you are already in trouble. That is when you need help, without interest or extra payment. You are trying to keep things together, not finding a way to lose it all faster.

Losing your job can only show you, the financial house of cards you have built for yourself. That is when the truth is revealed, living and spending like things will never change, is a way to build a nice house of cards. When you are building anything, you need a strong foundation. Without a strong foundation, you will just be gone with the wind, with nothing to hold on to. You have to live with the best in mind but prepare for the worst.

The idea that your job is secure will have you acting a certain way, living for the moment, not preparing for the future. It is never too late to clean up your act and start preparing for the future. By cleaning up your act, I mean getting out of consumer debt. Getting rid of some of your payments, paying certain items faster so you can enjoy them without payments. And Lastly, have a real safety net, I mean to have money you can use in time of financial trouble that will not require a payment or interest after you have used that money.

Simple actions steps to get you started. If you have credit card debt, stop spending and buying using credit. Try to lower your interest rate, by asking them to lower it, or switching your account to a card that has a lower interest rate. Find a way to lower your bills, you might have to stop some services you aren't really using. Save at least one month of your paycheck. This way you are at least one month ahead. Save every dollar you can to start paying that debt down. This way if anything happens you have fewer bills and payments.

If you have no debt, you have to find a way to save as you have never saved before. You have the option of finding the strength to save now, while you are employed or losing everything if you lose your job later. Have the money and not use it, is better than not having it and needing it. You will sleep better at night knowing regardless of what happens to your income, you have months saved. It depends on who you are, but having 3 months is a good place to start, nothing is preventing you from having 6 months or a year.

There are no rules, you make your own rules, but having nothing is a recipe for disaster. That money can only be spent if a real emergency happens. It is not for spending or buying the latest gadgets or toys. The way you have to see it, is 'this is how my bills will be paid if I get laid off.' It is your 'sleep well at night account' when your paycheck is gone. Because you don't know how long it will take to find another job. Making sure you keep everything you have during this time is the place to start. Security is what you have saved, not what you expect will always come, and will never stop coming.

SECOND STORY

Unlimited time, the perception that we will have time at an undetermined later date. The idea of doing it tomorrow, in this case doing something tomorrow that can be done or started today, is the illusion. For most of the things that can have a real impact on our lives, it can be started and finished in a day. The failure to get started is enough to kill our chances of even doing what we think is important to us tomorrow. What you spend your time doing is what is a priority for you. Because one thing we have the ability to choose is what we do with our time.

The good thing about life is that time is the same for everyone across the board. No one gets more time in a day for any reason. We all get the same amount of time to do what we want to do. Yet some of us have no time, or so we say, and lack time to do the most important things that can affect our future. What is important and not urgent is put to the side until it is almost too late and that is when we start to scramble, trying to get things done. The sooner you start, the less stress you will have and the faster the goal can be reached regardless of what that goal is.

We have this idea that life is short, and we will have time to start saving later on. Now it is time to enjoy life and get the things we want. We live like we have unlimited time and when we start saving later we will have enough time to reach our goals. If we took the time to think about it, we would see it is much easier to start saving earlier, put less money in and stretching it over a longer period of time is easier than when we are closer, to stop everything else and try to put everything we have towards retirement.

Some of us are trying to live a life based on how we were when we were in school. Some of us enjoyed all the time we had before it was time to do a project, study for an exam until the last minute and some of us would only finish the project the same day or finish studying that morning before going to school. This might have worked for some of us in school. Waiting for the last minute when it comes to your life is risky because you have no repeat in life. Since we say we only live once, why risking having to work when all you want to do is stop working and enjoy whatever time you have left?

We have more and more time. We do only live once, but the life expectancy is becoming longer and longer and prices do not seem like they are going to be any cheaper than they are today. Delaying is only putting you at risk or having to live the last part of your life struggling. Depending on when you retire, you might have 20 years or more in retirement. If you are going to live 20 years or more on investments and what you saved for the rest of your life, you need to start as soon as possible. The only person that will care about your living situation at retirement is you.

I remember when I was younger; all I could hear was people talking about retiring at 55 years old and living on a pension. Now it is more like retire at 67 years old with no pension and you have to save enough to make it last, which is hopefully longer than your life expectancy. If you fail because you started too late, all you can do is keep working and doing so until who knows how much longer. We cannot afford to wait to get started. Getting started now is our only option. If you do not get started now you will regret not having started sooner. The earliest you can start is now, the past is gone and in the future, you will regret not having started today when you read those words.

The idea you only live once is good when you are young and do not know how much time you have left. So living life to the fullest means spending it all and having a good time. After doing this for years and having time pass you by and not preparing for the future, the worst that can happen for someone who only lives in the moment, is not have anything in the future when they can no longer work in their field and have to work a minimum wage job serving people who are young enough to be their grandchildren.

Let's play a game, imagine what would be the outcome if you lived that way your whole life. You lived in the moment, always had the latest gadgets, waited for that job with a big income to start saving for retirement, always enjoyed changing cars every few years. Now you are approaching 50 and you realized you want to retire soon and you have no interest in working much longer. You decide to start saving at 50 but you have bills to pay and loans to pay off, payments on the car and a balance on your credit cards. How much can you save now at 50 since you never started and have barely or no wiggle room now?

Let's say you knew you were going to live for 80 years and you want to stop working at 65. This means your savings and investments would need to last you 15 years and during those 15 years, you would still want to enjoy your last moments here, right? If you haven't been able to have an emergency fund of a minimum of 3 months of your take-home pay. I say three months of your take-home pay because, if you lose your job and all you can do during those 3 months is pay for your bills, chances are you will not be as cheerful as having exactly what you were making. If you were not able to save this minimum during all your working life, how can you live for 15 years of retirement?

We think life is short but for most of us, life will be long. Meaning we are living longer and longer and when you live longer, your need for money can only be long term. If your need for money is long term how can you even imagine you can reach those goals short term by spending decades of working wages without having any to set aside? Reaching those long-term goals without those decades of wages will be impossible. I do not know about you, but working all my life and still having to work past retirement just so I can survive is not what I am interested in, as I get older.

Time can be our best friend but it can also be our worst enemy. For time to be our best friend, we need to start planning today for our later days. When we do so, time is our best friend, and what we need to save is much smaller because it is spread over time. Time can be our worst enemy if we just waste it and just watch it pass by. If you do not catch some of it by keeping some of the income you received, you will not remember where it went you will only see that you do not have enough in the present. Time can be used to empower us and help us reach our goals.

If we really wanted to see how long it would take us to reach a financial goal we would sit down use an online calculator and calculate how long it would take us to reach it. We would do it for both sides, let's say you decide you will have a good time from 25 to 45, just enjoy life and not even think about the future. You would then calculate how to reach your goal from, let's say 45 to 65 and how much you would need to save during that time. It might sound like a good idea you get 20 years of fun and 20 years of being conscious about savings.

The problem with this is we cannot predict the future. What we are making now does not mean we will make more. If you lose your job and all you can find is something that pays less. Whatever rate of savings you calculated would not work. The thing is, most of us do not even plan we just live, spend and wake up one day remembering do not want to work forever and if you want more than the tiny amount the government might give you, you need to have your own money set aside. I say might, because we do not know if and how much those governmental programs will be able to give us and whatever they give, will be not enough to live on.

Time is the most precious thing we have on this planet, yet we act like it will last forever. I feel, as I am getting older, time just fly by. One reason for this could be when you are doing a job you cannot stand and just want to be free. All you do is want your time at work to go by fast and somehow by magic you want your evenings to last longer. Most of us live for the evenings and weekends and for our vacation days. Living like this can only accelerate our perception of time being fleeting because we spend the week not wanting to be somewhere, then comes the weekend that seems to go by too fast and we look forward to the next weekend on Monday morning.

This cycle of always looking forward makes us miss and not use whatever time we have left after work. That time is being used to relax and decompress from our day. If all we do is decompress and relax after the day we do not have time to even think about how fast time is passing, let alone starting to plan for it. It is sad that most of us just enjoy our evenings and weekends and our vacations, but yet do not plan for not having to work for all our lives.

We always have a time in mind for when we will get started. For some reason that time is always in the future. What you plan and keep in the future will never come. The reason is, how can you get closer to a moving target? If every day that target is moving how can you reach it? If we all have the same amount of time during the day, when do some people take the time to plan and prepare for how they want their lives to be? It is done after work and on the weekend, the good thing when you put something on a calendar and have reminders of that time you are then able to sit down and do what needs to be done.

You can start changing your future by simply putting a date on when you will do something. You have to make sure the date you choose is close enough so you do not lose momentum and the desire to do things. You need to act as soon as possible when the motivation is there. Trying to do something when you are not motivated is practically impossible for most of us. When we are excited about something, and before we get distracted is the time to act. If you let that moment pass who knows when that idea will cross your mind again.

We have so much to think about and do during our everyday life. We spend our life living and doing things in the moment, while never raising our heads to see where we are headed. Seeing where you are headed is fairly simple, imagine you keep doing what you are doing now and what you have been doing. The only thing that can happen is more of the same and more of the same can be good, or bad, depending on where you want to go.

No one ever says "I want to make sure I work pass retirement age and work at a minimum wage job after age 67 with teenagers and young adults as colleagues." This eventuality happens slowly and gradually by just living and paying the monthly bills and not thinking about anything else. When you just focus on your life as you are living it, there is no way for you to be prepared for anything else. If someone would come to you and tell you where the road you have been driving on would lead, I am sure you would make some changes. Changes drastic enough to change your destiny from poor and working, to comfortable and enjoying life.

Living longer was always something to look forward to. You get to spend time with your children and grandchildren. Having more time is a source of joy and hope and being able to do everything you always wanted to do and having the time to do so. What has changed is, when you are the one who takes care of your financial life and you do not know how, and you are at the end of your working life, you worry about out-living the little, if any, the money you have saved. That longevity perspective is more something to worry about, than something to celebrate.

There are a few things you are in control of in this life and that is, your time and how you spend your money. The two combined can give you more choices. The more you have, the more you will want. If you have a lot of free time, you will want more. If you have money, you will want more money. No one is hoping to have less and struggle when we are at our most vulnerable. What you do now will impact how you live in the future. We cannot just think for the now, we have to always keep the future in mind. When some of the actions in the present are geared to help you have a better future, that, in my opinion, is living life to the fullest.

Living life just for the present is not living life to the fullest. Because if you spend all you have in the present, you will be struggling in the future. When you are struggling, you are not living life to the fullest. The only way living for the moment works, is if you are planning to work for the rest of your life. If so, than this is the way to go. But, if, like most of us, you want to stop working one day and enjoy the fruits of your labor, you need to have some fruits. If you have no fruits because all your fruits were eaten decades ago, what will you enjoy?

The goal is to do both, enjoy the fruits of your labor in the present, but have some left to enjoy in the future. Otherwise you might have to labor until you die, if you didn't save any of the fruits of your labor. You can always work to make money, spend it all and go back to work. Or, you can work, save and invest, because some day what you saved and invested allows you to never have to work again. The decision is yours; if you want to always have to work to have money, that is an option, but also know you have another one. If you are going to work and if you hate working, the best thing you can do is save and invest enough so you no longer need to work and you can enjoy your life doing what you want regardless of money.

THIRD STORY

The desire to be like others, finding what is normal and doing it. Normal is safe because no one is judging you and no one has any strong opinion about what you are doing. Since others are doing it, you have a false sense of safety. You feel because everyone or almost everyone is doing it, it has to be the way. Without even thinking about it, you feel that it is the best way, because if there were a better way everyone would be doing it. Everyone doing something only means most of us look at what others are doing and if everyone is doing it, we feel that's the way to go.

Is the right way to go, what is normal? Meaning because everyone is doing it, this has to be it. How to really tell which way is the way to go? There should never be only one way to do something. There has to be always a few ways of doing anything. Just have someone do something, and do not tell them how to do it, and you will see they will find a way to do things you never thought of. When you tell them how to do something and plan things out for them, that is when you have taken away their natural ability to come up with a solution.

We all have a way of doing things unique to us. Our way of thinking is also different from each others. This is one reason when you ask someone an open question you can have so many answers that you never thought of. Yes, there are a few of answers that will be similar, but not all of them will be the same. That is the beauty of being human, everyone thinking differently and deciding what is the best way for them to do certain things. Choosing what is best for you and your family is the greatest power you have. Just going with the crowd or where most are going, is where we are most vulnerable.

When you are in a riot or any big group of people, you see people who would not behave in a certain way normally, act that way in the situation. When we are in a group and there are a few taking the lead or starting something, we tend to just follow and go with the flow. When we go with the flow we have not taken the time to think about it. When you do not take the time to think about it and just do what others are doing, how can you learn anything when it goes where you never expected it to go. Some of us have less control and act out when we are not happy about certain things. When you are present when others are acting out and those are the leaders, what you were normally able to control you will feel justified letting loose.

The approval of others comes in so many ways. When you have someone sharing their discontent with a system, events or political party and others are just there applauding and agreeing with cheers and other outward actions, you will feel if that was a time to let loose and act now would be the time to do so. How can you tell the ones acting out the most are really motivated by the event they are acting out against? Not all times but certain times those people acting out are people who love when things get a little crazy and use it for their own entertainment.

If we take the example of rioting because your sports team lost. Yes, you can justify your actions and come up with reasons to be mad, but it is just a game and not your life. So going in the streets and make noise and vandalizing property does not change the outcome of the game. As for the people that were not there at the game, they have no idea why your team losing can cause so much damage, and would rather not have so many people passionate about sports. Being affected when your team loses a championship and rioting because of a loss can seem normal for some, but taking free stuff by breaking storefront windows does not. I do not see how the two are linked.

There maybe a few people thinking, this is going too far. I do not want to get caught or end up in jail or associated with this crowd. When you see others getting free stuff and you are in a bind and you see them getting away with it, you are potentially more inclined to give it a try because somehow you think they cannot catch everyone and somehow you think you will not be one of the people that are caught. When and if you do get caught the reality of your own personal consequence will show you how following the crowd was a bad idea.

If you are the only one or part of the group who are living with the consequence of one action because you followed the crowd you will regret it and be bitter because some never had to deal with the consequences of their actions. When it is time to pay a price and that price cannot be paid, as a group it has to be paid on an individual level this is when you notice this was not you and that it was a bad idea. The problem is we are often asleep until it is too late, we just act, not thinking of what can happen or where this road can lead us and the fact that nothing happened before does not mean nothing will.

If you do something for years and never get caught you will tend to believe nothing will come of it and you can continue. The problem with this newfound confidence is that it is based on past results and not getting consequences is only an indication that consequences are coming. Whenever we do something we have consequences, some take much longer than others, but one day it will all come crashing down depending on what you were doing and thought you could get away with it forever. For certain things we just act, do it because that is what everyone is doing.

Who is everyone? There is never everyone, there are always different groups. The simple way to expose this everyone theory is, there are rarely if ever, any statistics about 100% of the respondents doing one thing and all agreeing with it. There are always different views, actions or behavior. Having a group of 100% of everyone doing something is rare, if not impossible. Yes, depending on what it is, we can see a very big percentage of the population doing something. That big number should scare you because when most of the population is doing something and that action happens to be wrong, a lot of people will suffer and lose it all.

How can you find out if what you are doing has an ultimate positive destination? Find out where the majority of the people doing the same actions are headed. Doing so is fairly simple. If everyone is doing something you can find older people who have done it and see where they ended up. Once you have done this, do not rationalize it and think that it is the way and everyone ends up there. There is always a small group doing things totally differently and that small group has a different destination. You spend time studying that small group, and not just accept one way of doing things.

I am only talking about actions that have nothing to do with how other humans are being treated. Actions that are legal and will not get you in any trouble with the law. Actions that are in your control and no one thinks about questioning. Actions that can affect your financial future. Just acting without thinking or seeing the full picture can only lead you to a place you do not want to go. In order to end up where you want, first you need to know where that is, and this has nothing to do with anyone one else.

When you are following someone you can only go where they are going. You can only stop where they have stopped. You can only see what they are seeing you cannot see other options that might be better, and better is based on where you want to go. Your actions should be based on where you and your family want to go. If the neighbor wants to go somewhere else, how can you follow him? When you have no destination, you can easily fall for following others. You will not even see that you are following others, because you are just on autopilot. You have heard and you are seeing people doing it one way so you just do it.

In order to be part of the group, even if you do not realize it, you are behaving like the majority is behaving. If no one is questioning or opposing your actions or thinking in any way shape or form that you are acting in a way that is not normal for them. If that is normal for them then you are just following what is normal and not rocking the boat with a different way of thinking and seeing the world. We are all different and do not have the same goals and we do not want the same things. It might look like we want similar things but there are ways of achieving them. The easiest way to see it, is we do not all wear the same clothes or have the same tastes when it comes to music.

The question is then, why are people who are so different, behaving the same way financially as a whole? How can it be that they have bought the same ideas and are following the same plan without knowing they are following a plan? Because if you do not have a plan you are planning to fail. One possibility of this is people are just following the advice given to them. Most of this advice is just repeated without even thinking about if it is still valid and where it will lead and the impact it has daily on our financial lives. We just do because it is the way it is done.

From what we can see, everyone is doing it. It might be everyone one we know, and come across, but it is not everyone. We have a small group of people that we know and look to, for what it normal. Those people might not have a clue of what they are doing and never paid any attention to it either, but are following the advice they got. If we all repeat and do the same thing, without someone thinking about it and it because just something automatic everyone is doing, we will not even think about it or question it. Only someone who did not get the programming or was awakened by someone else who woke up knows better. The best way to wake up is have your life change, because if you keep going and nothing happens, you will not see the real flaws of that plan.

We all have a plan, things we do to get what we want. If you did not sit down and write that plan, how can you know where it will lead you? The good thing about money when it comes down to it is that it is math and math has no opinions, it can only show you the truth. You do not have to agree and it does not need your permission. What can happen is you can see a major flaw in some of your actions when it comes to money and how you are spending it. For you to see before experiencing it you will have to crunch the numbers. If you do not do so, chances are you will learn it all too late. If we just follow advice and do what is done and advertised to us, we will end up where they want us to end up.

If you do not have a plan for your money, someone else will have a plan for it. When someone has a plan for you, it almost always has their best interest in mind, not yours. No one will care about your money the way you do. When you are out struggling and when it is gone you will be the only one living with the consequences. If we are the ones who will experience it, we should think about it a lot more than we do. Because for most of us we just act. We just follow a normal progression and that normal progression leaves us with nothing.

The normal progression is for failure. We all want more money but what will we do with more money? For most of us, we will spend more. I remember the first real job I got, by this I mean working in a field I studied in. I was taking the bus there and walking 2 kilometers to work, after getting of the bus, I remember that figure because I used it to complain and justify the normal spending progression. I remember it like it was yesterday one day after work and walking back to the bus stop. I have had it, after one of my colleagues talked about how long of a walk it was.

I was like she is right, it is a long walk, and having to do it every day, those conversations had been going on for a while but that day it was my breaking point. I do not know if the bus came late or something but I remember going to the car dealership and wanting to get a car because I was tired of walking and taking all my time riding the bus. I had just started my job and did not have much money but was making enough to get a car loan of $13000 or something, which was a lot for me. I remember being worried about not being approved for the loan. When I was, it was like winning the lottery, but with payments.

The first thing I did without thinking about it, is justify what was fine and had been all my life. I was taking the bus to school and to work I was working after school and that never bothered me. I was fine and did not mind it. The moment I started making money is when I saw a problem where there was none before. That problem was solved by spending more because I was making more. It never crossed my mind to save for a car or the impact of the payments on my life if my situation changed. All I saw was here and now and what I needed was to stop walking. It was not a plan, but just acting without thinking ahead or any of the consequences.
Everything was fine until one day it all changed and that action was exposed.

When my financial situation changed and I was not able to pay for the car, that is when I noticed the burden of having a payment. If I would have saved a few months or a year I would have had savings and would have been fine. But now I had a car payment, insurance and no income. That is really when I noticed that having payments felt like having shackles around my ankles and limited my options and made life harder. What I thought would solve problems, which was just waiting for the bus and walking created new ones I did not know existed.

Most of us make financial mistakes and one of the big ones is increasing spending when we have more income. If more income meant more savings we would be a lot richer than we can even imagine. When we buy something using a loan or credit, the price we pay for it is a lot more than the price tag. We have no real idea how much more we pay; we have the price of the loan and the amount with taxes but what about the monthly interest. If we did simple math and noticed if we saved and were patient enough we would see that paying for the price tag with the taxes is the cheapest amount we can pay.

We can afford it over time, we just get to have it today and paying a lot more for it. It is amazing how we can pay a payment but have a hard time saving that money ourselves. It is the same money, we are the same person but we see the bank payment as an obligation. If we saw ourselves as more important than the bank we would be able to save and pay for the price of the car in the example without paying any extra for it. What is the point of negotiating the price if you are going to pay more for it anyway? When you pay for something in full on that day it is the cheapest price you will ever have.

There is also the trap of zero interest or low interest. Yes, you do not pay more on the money you are loaned, but you are paying so much for something that will not have the same value when you drive it off the lot and will drop significantly in the first 4 years. Yes, the loan you took is the same and you will not be paying more than what is actually taken, but since the car will be worth so much less in a 4 years. You are paying for something that is worth so much less. That is where you lose all your money; buying something that loses so much value it is a bad idea.

When it comes to money and spending money, it is either something you use to reach your goals and dreams or something you use to do what others are doing. When you just do what others are doing and want to be included and be part of the group even when you cannot afford it, you are the only suffering while the others might be able to afford it and not be affected by it. Staying honest with yourself and being able to say no when you have other plans with your money is a nice place to start. Make sure you arrive where you want to and not were others are going...

FOURTH STORY

Luck is the reason why someone is living the life they are living. When you say luck is the reason someone has anything, what you are doing is quitting before you even get started. You are basically saying, "he is lucky, I am not, therefore there is nothing I can do regarding the way my life is. If I was lucky like that person is, my life would be much different." Luck implies little to no personal responsibility in the events that are happening in our lives. Luck is often seen as someone living a normal life, behaving like everyone else and all of sudden they are taken away from the grind and are now living the life of their dreams. A life most of us can only dream of, since we see that way of life as so far fetched, luck is the easiest explanation.

If we look at the basic lucky event of winning the lottery, even then, some action was needed for that person to win. That action might have been taken only once, or for years. Not many of us would play for years in the hope of maybe winning one day. Most of us see it as impossible; even if it might be impossible from a mathematical standpoint it is still possible. Even the tiniest chance can make it happen for those who decide to play, whether it is once, or over a longer period of time. The desire to even give it a chance is how one has a chance.

If you do not even play, your chance is zero. You have zero chances of winning. When you have zero chances of winning and someone you know or someone you see on television wins, you feel they are lucky. Yes in this instance they are, but before they were able to win, they had to purchase a ticket, be willing to lose and still do it anyways. They understood "if I do not play, my chance of winning are impossible." What makes your chance impossible is when you do not even try. When people play the lottery their odds of winning are one in millions.

We are somewhat skeptical about so many things and we tell those people they are wasting their money and they should be saving it. Playing for fun is not a bad idea, but do not make it the only way for you to reach a financial goal or the only way for you to have a lot of money come into your life. When you play just for fun with a small amount that has no real impact on your financial future, then it's not a big deal. Just like the person that plays every week, we do not know if they will be part of the lucky ones who took action even if this action simple as purchasing the ticket.?

There is no luck without action, the bigger the odds the smaller the actions. Winning the lottery does not require much more than taking the time to go stand in line to buy the ticket and having the money to do so. It does not require any major effort, time, and commitment to do so. Most of us see this plan as failing until someone wins one day. When a person who is close to us wins, somehow we, for a minute or two, think we should play or should have been playing. Having that person just leave work and us staying there is something most people do not want to experience.

When I was younger one of my colleagues won the lottery, she was nice enough and decide to treat us to lunch. We were a small office of six people. I was happy with her nice gesture but I noticed that some of my other colleagues were somehow expecting more. She soon left and stop working. I remember how people were wondering how much she won and how life would be different if it would have happened to them. One thing I know, I did not play and I am still not playing now.

Fast forward to today, as I am writing this, my colleagues play every time there is a big amount. Most of them just play for the reason of not being the only one left behind. Just the idea of everyone leaving and moving on is hard to even imagine. It is their major reason for playing. Is the lottery the only way one can avoid the grind of working at something that they do not enjoy and would leave the day they do not need money. The real indicator is if you love what you are doing, would you still do it every day if you had millions? If not then you need to find a way out.

Winning the lottery cannot be our only way to early retirement. Because most of the lottery winners take an early retirement from something they did not enjoy, and go do things they love doing. Thinking of other ways to live the life we want to live, without one big amount coming into our lives is not as impossible as it may seem. One way to do this is by elimination, since most of us are not aspiring to be actors, athletes, musician, or entertainers, what are we left with? What options do we have? If you were not born into a family that is rich, what can you do to live a life of riches, or just a more comfortable life? It all depends on what your goals are and most importantly, what you think is possible.

There is something that has been said and is often repeated to us, Business is risky. 90% of businesses fail within 5 years, therefore why even get started? Based on my lottery example business is more of a sure thing than the lottery, the percentage is much higher. What we should be looking at is 10% of the people doing it, succeeding. Do we have 10% of people playing the lottery winning? Of course not, but people are still willing to give it a try. The reason people are not willing to give business a try is because of the size of the investment when it comes to time, money and skills.

Anyone can buy a lottery ticket, but can everyone build a successful business? Does everyone want to take the risk and the effort needed to do so? Not only do you need the skills, invest the time and the money, but you also need to have something different to offer in this global market. If you do not have those as a minimum, business is out for you. If you think about it, everyone working a job, has a job because someone started a company and that company is still standing. It is an easy way to see how businesses create more wealth and have a better chance of success if you are incline to do so, or if it is something you wish to do. But since we are all different, not everyone wants to be a business owner.

When it comes to businesses of any kind, the amount of time and work and dedication is not something we can even imagine or predict. When you see someone sell their businesses for millions, they are not lucky, it was a long and hard process that most of us are not even willing to do, or even desire to get started. When it comes to the potential outcome of building a business somehow our focus is on the ones that failed and not on the ones that are a success story. If you have a job, your company is somewhat a success story because it is still open in this economy.

Luck is created by events and the bigger the risks, the bigger the rewards. If you do not take any risks you will not have any big rewards. If all you do is spend everything you make, you cannot have any big rewards. If you do not have the mind of an entrepreneur your chances of mass success is limited. If you want something different than your coworkers have, you will have to do something different. You can be considered lucky for someone unemployed who cannot find anything. You can be seen as doing well by someone who makes less money.

When it comes to you, you are involved in the luck that shows up in your life. If a business is not for you, there is no way someone will come to your job and buy your position for millions. When you take no risk your luck is limited to the potential bonus at work or a raise by the company. Those who have luck had to sacrifice for years in order to have the big one. Think about this, what have you built for someone to come around, evaluate it, and say this is worth millions? The person showing up at some point can be predicted by the size of what you are building.

Someone coming and buying what you have built is not luck, because without you building something, no one will come and offer you millions for just being there. We can see it as hard work paying off on a massive scale. If you see it as a job, you have done such an amazing job that people with money start noticing you. After noticing your work, they love it so much they want to make it theirs and the only way to make it theirs fast, without any effort, is to buy you out. It is the same thing as you buying a condo from a builder.

The builder is not lucky; he took the time and effort to build the condo building. You found your way to his building, noticed the condos and decided it was what you were looking for and decide to purchase it and make it yours. If you simplify business being bought this way for millions, you can see that the business builder was not lucky, but he created his luck by creating something that is worth buying. Not only did he create something and is part of the 10% that succeeded, but he also went beyond that. Since we are not all builders, there is something we can all do to create our luck.

We live in a biased society; we never see the full picture of anything. We only see highlights; if you missed a sports game and you are watching the news you will see a few minutes of the best moments of a game. What we see is the end result, we have no idea what it took and we, therefore, assume that person is lucky. I am sure someone who worked harder than everyone else to achieve a goal would be offended by having their hard work called luck by people who did not do the work. When we see someone sell their companies for millions we just see the millions, we do not how long it took them, the sacrifices they had to make to reach that goal. Hard work and sacrifice does not sell, we only see the results.

When you only see the results you have no idea how long it took. The end product does not tell you what it took to create it. Those stories do not help us; they paint a false perception of reality. If they would take the time to talk about the years of work, getting up early and going to bed late, driving a very old car to put all the money on the goal, never going out on vacation and not taking time off. We would have a better picture of what it takes, and most of us do not have the desire to do all this without any guarantee of making it. There are no guarantees.

When we see everything is a result of actions and the bigger and more complex, the more actions it took. We can see those results are not luck and cannot be looked at as luck. Luck can be seen as how big your harvest will be when it comes to farming, but you still had to plant and take care of the fields for months and bad weather can make it all go away and you have no crops to harvest, but you still did the work. You can do the work and have nothing to show for it. We see bad news about people's lives on TV, but when it comes to failing you are doing it alone.

Why do people want to come and join you when you are succeeding? Where is everyone when you are struggling to reach your goals? There are no cameras and no public attention when someone is going through a hard time. When someone makes it, everyone wants to be in and want their share. Funny how people feel entitled to something just because they knew you for years, never helped and may have even made fun of your goals and dreams, seeing them as impossible. But the moment it works and you are living a different life, everyone comes out of the woodwork and want to be helped. But who helped you when you had problems and was trying to do the impossible?

If there is any advice I can give you, its support other's dreams, not in the hope of getting something, but as a way to see magic happening. When you see magic happens for someone close to you and you were there for them, you have a front row seat of what it took. You now have more chance of success at what you want to do. The principals of success are often the same, only the goal is different. Help someone, so you can believe in what is hard to believe in.

When it comes to you and your own dreams, you are the dreamer, regardless of what you want to do. It can be going for a promotion at your job, you have to see what the people who are in that position have and acquire it when possible. You created luck, meaning attention by someone else seeing your skills or what you have built by working either on yourself, a project, a business or in school. If you do not work and go beyond what everyone else is doing you will be where everyone else is. My definition of luck is, therefore, the result of work that is beyond what is common. When you are in the middle no one sees you.

We are noticed when we are on top or at the bottom. Where you end up is based on your own actions, no one can make you or force you to stay in any of the major groups. When you are on top, there are fewer people and you get noticed more, and for some reason that is weird to me, people tend to be jealous. Funny how no one is jealous of what helped someone be on top, they just want that position. When you do more, you get more. It all depends on what you are focused on, my focus has been what can most of us do, we can work, or not, to be on top.

When you are in the middle, you do just enough to stay employed and you do not go beyond. You show up, do your work enough so your boss leaves you alone, then you go home and enjoy the rest of your day. If you use my definition of luck, beyond the result of which is; going beyond what is common, there is no way you can be lucky by not going beyond and doing more. You will most likely stay there or get fired if there comes a time to cut some positions.

When you are at the bottom, you do less than the minimum required, you are noticed too, but not for good reasons. You will most likely be the first to go in a tough economy, but for this to happen your boss needs to be aware. You can be at the bottom, meaning doing less work and still get away with it and your colleagues can be the only ones to know. You might think you are living the life, but chances are you will not be lucky for long because of not going beyond the amount of work the others are doing. You can be seen as doing enough work to be in the middle with everyone else.

No one gets big results without any actions that are above the ordinary. If you want your financial life to be above the ordinary, you will have to do things differently. One of those things that everyone can do is save. Yes, many have saved, invested their income without starting a business or winning the lottery to be able to retire with more than they earn their entire lives. This is not luck, but decades of savings and investing. This is one action that anyone can do with enough work and dedication that can create a result others might want to call luck.

Luck is not there when there is no discipline, hard work and dedication. Hard work does not always mean physical work; it could be mental work and coming up with ideas no one ever thought of, or solving a problem for people that makes their lives more enjoyable. If you want luck to come into your life you will need to find something you are willing to do, stick to it and focus until you reach your goal. With more work your results tend to be greater, the more you save now, the more you will have and sooner you will be able to reach your financial goals..

FIFTH STORY

I am a good person; therefore I deserve more than I currently have. The fact that I am good, honest and a hard worker means that I deserve more out of life. "I should have more", when you think that way where is the more supposed to come from? Who can give you more? Who is in control of what everyone has, and gives them more than others? Do we have someone over us deciding how much we get and how much our neighbors get? Why do some people have more while others can barely make ends meet? If we all started the same, why do some end up at different destinations?

What I mean by starting at the same place is, we often are in the same graduating class, while a few end up having a lot more than the rest of the class, the others do not. Who do we call for justice? Why do we need justice? Why do we want what others have? Why do we assume we are a better person than they are and we deserve more? Deserving is entitlement, something we should have, regardless of our actions, and behaviors. Something we should get just for being alive. When you think of it this way, you will see what we deserve is very slim while everything is our own making.

We are all worth the same when it comes to being humans. No one is worth more or their lives are worth more. We all have human rights and there's a list by the United Nations to show how we should be treated and the freedoms we all have. As humans, no one deserves anything more than the others. If someone is deserving, it means there is someone in control of the supply and sharing it. It can also mean someone will go grab what is yours and give it to you. It might be a lawyer, or the government. When it comes to our normal lives, what we deserve is what we worked for, not who we are.

You do not get to eat because you are hungry; everyone deserves food and shelter as a minimum, which is required for basic human survival. If people who are starving do not get food, are they not deserving of food? If someone sleeps outside and has nowhere to be sheltered from the weather, does that person not deserve a home? We live in a society where even the basic needs for survival need to be paid for. Deserving in the world we live in implies you can afford it or are able to pay constantly for it. This shows the flaws in deserving if you are hungry and have no money, whom can you go see to feed you without having any money?

Can you go to the grocery store and take what you need for survival? If you can't, then what we think we deserve in this current society does not mean much. Since we are not all producers of everything we need and no one person produces everything, we need to purchase what we need from others. That transaction, or purchasing what we need, requires a form a payment. If you cannot pay, you cannot have it legally and with peace of mind. We live in a world where nothing is free, not even food and maybe one day water will not be free either. Those are basic needs for everyone.

What we feel we need and are deserving of, depends on where we are financially and where we live in the world. If you are living in a third world country, what you feel you deserve is different than what someone living in a first world feels they deserve. When your basic needs as a human being are not met your entire focus is on survival. When you are hungry it is hard to change your focus from food. When you are well fed and you have a place to sleep, that is when you start to add to what is needed for your life to be normal, and normal, is in relation to others close to you.

I was born in a third world country; I was born in Haiti and moved to Canada when I was 7 years old. For me it was a different world in Canada, everything seemed weird. There was too much control and not enough freedom. One thing I noticed is in third world countries, where they do not even have water to drink and to stay alive, they have to walk miles to bring some dirty water home to drink. I noticed here they had pools, fountains and water all over the place for entertainment and art. I never understood how that can be, but when you can drink all you want, you have other needs and desires and in this example, water and looking pretty in a fountain is one of them.

Since we can all agree we all need water to stay alive, that is something we all deserve. Yet people die without enough food and water, while here we have nice fountains and throw away food that we do not find attractive enough in our supermarkets. If we think we deserve more, then everyone should have at least the bare minimum, otherwise we are doing the same thing that some consider that the rich are doing, which is taking more and having more than others. To someone in a third world country everyone in a first world country is doing better than them and are considered rich.

When you feel poor and feel you deserve more and you want to feel rich, all you have to do is take a plane to a country poorer than yours and you will see you are not doing too bad. It is all in relation to where you are in the world. If traveling to a place in which your money was worthless and everything was more expensive than it was at home, you would think about it longer or save for it longer. When you are traveling, you also show how much you are willing to spend; going down south on the beach is much cheaper than traveling to Europe. One will make you feel poor, while the other will boost your self-esteem and make you feel you are doing pretty well.

We are doing better than we can see. We live in a society where wealth and riches is shown to us everywhere we look. We see someone making millions just for playing sports and we say we think we deserve more than our current salary. We see someone making millions for playing or acting and we think we should make more. What we often miss is those require some skills that we might not have. They might be looking for a certain type that is not us. Those people are seen as an investment. When someone is paid millions, it is because they will make the organization a lot more money. When a movie star is paid 20 million and the movie makes 400 million we can see that it was a good investment, people wanted to see that actor. When a player is paid millions of dollars and millions of people are willing to go see him play and buy his shirt, we can see why this player was paid millions. He made more money for the organization than you do for yours.

We have our worth as a human being and we have our worth and what we deserve in the market place. What we deserve at work is based on our value, a value that is always changing based on the skills we have and what we have learned. When you have minimum skills, you are paid minimum wage. The wage is not the problem because there are other jobs that pay more. For you to be paid more you will need to improve what you can do and the value you have within the company. The more people that can do what you do, easily, without much skills, the less you will be paid. It does not require much skill to flip burgers, or stack up shelves. Anyone can do it.

For you to deserve more when it comes to income, you will need to be different and have more skills to bring to the table. There is also the question of how many other people have that same skill set or education. If there is not much demand in an industry and you have a diploma in it, regardless of its level, you might find yourself not working in what you are trained for because there are too many graduates and not enough jobs in that field. You might have been told how much you deserve or will make when you are done school, but if there are more graduates than jobs, you will have to do something else. And most likely it might pay less than you were expecting and it could be something anyone with a high school diploma can do.

What we deserve when it comes to income is based on how rare our skills are or what we have to offer as well as how big the demand for those skills. If there were a lot of jobs, but only a few graduates, companies would compete for you and would come and get you in school before you are even done. That used to be common practice for some fields, it might still be, but not like it was before. Now there are too many graduates with only a few jobs. The companies get to choose while everyone else who wasn't chosen has to find another way to live and pay the bills or loans they might have.

You can have an amazing degree, have studied hard to achieve it, but if there are lots of people with that same diploma, and the number is too high compared to the demand of companies hiring people with that diploma, you will be out of luck. It is not only what you are studying, but also the needs of the market place and where that market place is heading that is important. Since you are planning to have a long career, what you know must be in, is something that will always be needed or present. If it is not then you will have to find something else to do. What is expected and feel you deserve when it comes to salary when we are in school, is based on the past and present, the future might change.

What you are being paid right now might not be what you feel you deserve, but since you are working for someone else, they get to choose how much they are willing to pay you. If you want a different pay you will have to be more valuable to that company, value meaning bringing them more than they are paying you and that at a different level. When you are able to do more, you are often paid more and promoted. If you are struggling with your job, you will not be more deserving in the eyes of the person paying your salary. There is no deserving or entitlement because that means someone else is in control.

If someone else is in control then what you feel you deserve is just your opinion while the one deciding is making the decision. If you are in control, then what you feel you deserve you don't need to ask anyone for it, you just go out and get it. You do not need to prove anything to anyone, or ask for it because you are the one making the decision. When you do not have what you want and need to ask someone else, they decide what you deserve. You don't and then you try to convince someone to give you more, while they feel you have enough or more than enough.

You are entitled to what you have created. The fact that someone good or bad has more does not really matter because you cannot ask them to give you what they have. You might want to take action and go take it from them, but when you do so you risk losing it all by ending up in jail. When you lose it all, is when you noticed how much you had in the first place. If you can find a way to be happy with what you have, you will find a solution for you to increase what you have based on your knowledge and skills.

If you feel you deserve more, you need to learn how others got more. Why are they making more, how come they can do certain things while you might not be able to do the same things. The good thing is there are so many books about people who have more and explain what they did differently and how you can do the same. If you want more, you are not limited to what you have or where you are, you can be more and therefore deserve more in the eyes of someone else who is in control. When someone controls your income they are in control of where you are, and how far you can go.

If you want to be in control of what you have, you need to be in control of your income. You can be in control of your income doing two things, spending less, and saving more. When you see someone with more, you do not know what they did to reach that level and be deserving of it. You can give yourself a raise by paying off some of your bills that alone will give you more money without asking for a raise. When we ask for a raise what we are really asking for is more income that is not dedicated to bills, income that is extra we can use for something else.

You might feel you deserve more money, and that decision might not be in your control, but what is in your control is the money you are already making. We often feel we need more money, but what will we do with more money. If more money means increased expenses, then more money will not solve anything, but will create more problems that will become obvious if our income lowers again. You might feel you want more and could use more, but did not notice that all you are saying is you want money you can use for something else, other than giving it to someone else.

How much of your money do you deserve? I am asking you, how much of the money you are making does the bank deserve? How much of the money you are making do those carmakers deserve? How much of your money does Apple deserve or any other cellphone company deserve? What you are doing, is saying you deserve more but you are giving what you have away. You are doing so many ways and ways that appear to be the way to do things, you do not even see and know how much is really going out in payments. You might see the number you have left and think it is too small but do you look at all the money that is gone?

Bills and expenses are the first place anyone can give themselves a raise without making more money. You deserve to keep more of your money. We often hear people say, "I work hard for my money" or "money is hard to make." Spending money seems to be a lot easier than making it. This is where you need to be vigilant and pay attention to what you are doing with what you have. This is where you are in control. This is where no one is forcing you to take a loan, pay high interest or make instalments on items. You make those decisions yourself; you are in control more than you give yourself credit for.

We often feel we deserve more money but very few of us keep most of the money we are making. A simple rule of money - if you do not have it anymore, you gave it to someone else and that person or company has more money and is growing while you are declining. We often hear people say, "I make this per year, I have this much take-home pay." We get angry and scream about taxes but we find a way to spend the rest, have it disappear and not know where it went. Were we not deserving of keeping some of that money or was something else more deserving?

You cannot have your cake and eat it too. You cannot say you want more money while everything you make is just gone. If all you make is gone and you have to wait until your next paycheck or are using credit to compensate, you are closer to financial trouble than you can imagine. The first thing you need to do is find yourself more deserving of your own money, more deserving than all the things you are drawn to by the clever marketing. You have to find a way to make sure you are more important than the next thing that comes out, otherwise, you will always chase a dream and will have nothing when you will need it the most.

We have a short memory; I have bought shoes I do not even remember that sounded so important. I remember buying a big screen television that I no longer own today. Let's not forget the cars I bought or the rent I paid, they are all gone and the money spend on them too. It would be too painful to do the math and see how much we have wasted. I say wasted, because since there will always be a newer and nicer version. Why spend so much on anything that can be easily replaced? When the dust settles, that is when we see it was not really worth it but at the moment is the most important thing. It was what we deserved but when it is gone we want more options and options comes with savings, without savings you are stuck..

SIXTH STORY

The only way you can learn something is in the classroom with a teacher and it has to be traditional and formal education. The education that is promoted is the end and be all we need to succeed and once we are done with that degree, we have learned all we need to, to have a successful and fruitful life. All we need is a degree and once we have that degree that is when the magic happens and that is what is needed for us to succeed. Without this, you will not be able to succeed and will be living in the poorhouse and in mediocrity the rest of your life.

This is also the one and only promoted and known way for us to learn and be educated. Once we have that education we feel we have everything that is needed. Now we wait for the magic to happen. When that magic does not happen we do not understand why. We did what we were told. When we are not able to find a job with that master key of life, we then are lost and some us just find a job in another field and let go. While others decide to add one more key to the keychain of success and go back to school and learn something else, but this time being a little more conscious about what is needed in the market place.

They chose their new field of study from what they see is missing, or the positions they see are available on the market but are not able to apply for now because they do not have what it takes yet. The problem in doing so, is you are going back to school for another 3 or 4 years depending on what job requires and you are trying to learn the skills for it and being marketable for. What if when you come out of school, those jobs are all filled and no longer exist? What then? Will you go learn something else that is needed in the present and be ready in the future when you are done with your degree?

This is a dangerous way of spending your life because at some point you need to start working and paying those student loans off if you had to take them. When you get a traditional loan for investing, you want to make sure that loan has some guarantee that you will make the money you invested, back. The problem with a degree is there are no guarantees of a good job once you are done. The people giving us schooling advice speak from their experience and while it did work for them back then, now the economy and the world are different. The problem nowadays is the world is changing more and more, but no one is really prepared, so the next best thing is to repeat what was done before.

As you may know, what was done before and the results that happened are not a guarantee for future generations. When you go from industrial age to the information age, then the information given to people has to be different. But since no one has lived it and we are all living it now and seeing how fast things are changing and how fast we all need to keep up, no one can predict what the future will hold. One thing that takes a long time to keep up is a society in general, because of how it was built. Being younger and having technology so young and always looking for the next best thing shows us that we cannot rely on the past ways anymore.

When you ask you, parents, who can barely use technology and that do not have your skills and understanding when it comes to technology and how fast the world is changing, when it comes to education, they will only tell you what they know and have used. There are only a few visionaries in our world and for most of us, it is not our parents. You can listen to their advice and follow it of course, but keep in mind that they were not born or raised in a rapidly changing world based on technology being the driving force.

We live in a world where technology is taking over everything we do and all areas of our lives. Based on what you are planning to do with your life, there are a few things you will need that you have not learned in school because it was impossible, as it was created after you were done your degree. Where you are going to be working they will be using technology already and if you are not qualified to use that technology, someone, else will, and that person will be your boss, someone younger with better skills and a better understanding of technology.

If I take my example, when I was younger I wanted to be a car mechanic or a computer technician. I thought about it, decided and looked at where the world was going and I saw it was not going to be manual labor. I then decide to go for a computer technician degree and it has made life so much easier and fun for me. Whatever job I would get, they would need someone with basic skills I was always on top and could even fix problems when they occurred. This gave me an instant edge over anyone else in my job. Even one of my bosses had me trained in the new software we were transitioning too.

My point is, there will be changes in technology and how things are done wherever you decide to work and what you decide to do. You will need to keep learning just to stay employed because when they change the software and how they do things you will have to be able to produce under new circumstances. The way you used to do something will not matter nor how good you were doing them. Your ability to change and grow fast will be the new master key you will need in order to just be employed. To be on top, you will need more and what you will need, will be self-education.

By self-education, I mean being self-taught or taught outside of work. Yes, you might say they have to train me on this it is their job but if you have not noticed, companies are more interested in people who already know how to use a computer system and their software, than to take the time to teach you. The simplest way to see this is, if you have been working for them for a while they will give you a chance and teach all the current employees, but anyone new will need to know how to use those systems before coming in or be computer literate before they even have an interview.

What this means is, they are more inclined to hire someone that has already been trained. This way they can focus on training that new employee on what needs to be done, meaning their job. Learning how to use a computer is something you need to know before you can learn the internal software and start being productive in your position. Regardless of what you are learning, or the job you will have, you will need strong basic computer skills. Those skills will bring you up to speed with the new kids out of college.

If you have been out of school for a long time and the position you had is gone, you will notice, if you have not yet, that most, if not all positions that are not manual labor, require you to be able to use computers with ease. When you can do that, you need to ability to learn fast what the job is and learning the company based software that you had no way of learning before being hired. Your ability to learn those and the rate you are learning them will decide if you are fit for the job when it comes to your new employer or even to yourself depending on how hard you find it.

Learning is a muscle, the more you learn on your own, the easier any transition will be. Companies have to change because when you are using computers and the company providing the operating system upgrades its version and does not offer any support for the old one. You are scared, as an employer and decide it is better to change for the new operating system. When you do so, it does not guarantee the software you were using will be compatible with the new operating system. That is when you have to replace what you were using and spend and train all your employees.

We live in a world where technology is changing so fast, that there is always a new camera with better features and more quality. There is always a new television with better quality and technology. We also have new technologies we did not have before, like portable electronics to enjoy our now digital entertainment. Let's not forget our smartphones that have replaced so many items we had before and those are changing so fast it feels they are coming with a better version every 6 months. Everything that is changing requires us to learn how to use it.

In the world we live in, your ability to adapt and learn and how fast you can do it, will give you an edge and will make sure you can always find work. Some of that learning can be done at home; you do not need to go to school to learn it. School means this has been around long enough for someone to write books and create a curriculum on it. Sometimes things are so new you need to learn it from experts that are doing it now and can show expertise. Anyone with enough skills can be your teacher if they can prove they have more skills than you and have the ability to teach.

No one will ask you where you learned to use the program. They will test your ability to use it. Before you even get an interview you will be tested on your skills, depending on the job you are looking for. They want to see if you can do the basics because they are not willing to teach you how to do it. The person that gets the job is someone that is ready to work.

You will need to be ready before you go for a new position or before you quit your job if you want to change the field you are in. You cannot wait to start learning when you need it because it will be too late.

The good thing with the world we live in is we can learn anything from home. We can go to the library grab a book on the subject and start learning without having to pay a dime. We can watch free videos online and get started. If you have a hard time learning by yourself, you can still find inexpensive classes that will teach you what you need to be marketable. We no longer need to spend 3 years learning things we will not need to be able to qualify for a job because the technology changed. The good thing when it changes is there are always books on the new technology teaching you how to use it.

I remember when I finished school, I used to hear people say I never have to do this again, meaning learning and going to school. If they kept that way of thinking, they are likely not able to find work today because a lot of the things we are using and which is required in order to work in most places, did not exist when we were in school. Depending on what you need, going back to school can be the best option if you need a degree, but when it comes to skills and a few new soft wares, you can do it at home or even take a class at night as some schools noticed that demand and offer those classes themselves now.

They offer those classes on nights and weekends but do not offer credits. When you see that even the school will teach you how to use a few software, but will not give you credits, what they are basically saying is you can learn this anywhere, you do not need a paper certificate or degree. You just need the skills and we are willing to help you with the skills if you pay us. They are basically using their reputation to teach you something anyone else could have learned on their own and on their own time.

Our new reality is we are not done when we finish our degrees. It is just the beginning of what we will need for the real world and our lives. When it comes to your job and career you will need to learn about technology and how to use computers, internet and anything else related to how your job will operate and be willing to learn something new, because they will not keep the same software for decades and will have to change because that software works on an operating system. If windows or Apple change their version and no longer support the older version they will have to change.

Even in your personal life, you will need to learn how to use technology. You will need to learn how to use your phone and other portable electronics. You will need to learn how to use your new television. You will need to learn how to use all the technology in your car. When it comes to the Internet at home, if you have it wireless you will need to learn how to secure it. Using just a simple password will not always be enough because it could be easily accessed. The good thing is for most of these you can have someone do it for you for at low to no cost.

There are other things we need to learn but never really paid attention to. Take the money, for example, money is a major one, and money is something so taboo no one talks about it. When no one talks about it, it makes us vulnerable because we have no idea what we are doing and we have no one to go see that can help us make better decisions. The only thing we are taught is to give it away to someone else and that person or institution will take care of it for us, and magically our money will make us more money.

We are taught we need to seek the help of experts, but do those experts have our best interests in mind? Or are they like us? Trying to earn a living and just doing their jobs? Their jobs can just be to offer us a few options that their boss told them to sell and in turn, the boss got that information from higher. Are they just repeating what they were told?

How can we know for sure what they are doing will help us? One of the ways would be to get advice that is not based on sales or seeking someone that has nothing to sell us but just letting us know how it is.

When it comes to your money or your financial future, no one will care more than you do. We see this with celebrities who focused on making the millions and gave that money away to someone else to take care of it and when that money disappeared, what can they do? Some try to sue the person who handled their money, but how often does that work? One of the things we were not taught is we have to understand money; we need to learn about money, we need the basics. It is obvious we do not know the basics because the way society is living will show you that we do not.

Since no one will care more about your money being gone than you will. You need to learn the basics of money. Just like technology, if you want to have a change, you need to learn that subject even if you do not like it or do not think it is for you. I am sorry to say that if you do not learn about it how it works, you will end up hurt and no one will come to the rescue. We live in a world where we are affected by our actions, our understanding and lack of understanding.

If you do not learn about money, chances are you will not have much and even if you make a lot of money like celebrities and athletes, chances are you will lose it all. That is, even if you give it to someone else with experience to handle it for you. Maybe you have not noticed when you have someone handle your finances, regardless of who it is, they always make money. They make money if you win; they make money if you lose money or even if you lose it all. What incentive do they have to make sure you win? They have no incentives, they are selling a product, once the sale is made what happens after does not affect them.

We live in a world where almost everything we walk into, is a business, and their main goal is to make a profit unless you walk into a place where they feed and clothe the poor. Otherwise, someone will sell you a product and that product when it is sold to you cannot be returned without losing money, the money you put in and money to get it out. When you see everything as a business, you will have a better understanding of how life really works. The bank is a business; they sell products and now charge you fees to use your own money. You pay for convenience, the easy access to your money. Someone came up with the idea of service fees per transactions, because before there were no fees and now all the banks copied this practice and charge fees.

If you have millions of clients and charge them a monthly fee, you can now see where the business comes in. It becomes like your gym membership if you have one, you pay when you go and you pay even if you do not. They have a major product that they sell, that some have called the equivalent of the cigarette of the financial world. That product is credit cards, this is a product that you do not need but have been sold on. Some of the banks even refer to their cards as products because they are. When you hear that banks are making so much profit, it is because they are businesses.

Businesses have products and the products they sell have to be advertised to us. That is why you see ads for credit cards. They are pushing their most profitable products. You get to have something today but will pay for it for years and you will pay a lot more than the price tag. You need that product to make this great deal happen. So we are sold on the practice of buying something today and then paying for it for months or years and to actually pay a lot more than the price tag, how is this a good deal? We are sold this product because some of us lack patience and we want it now.

Lack of patience is not free; it is charged with high interest and fees. The more they can get you in debt the better it is because you cannot pay it in full, and you will pay just minimum payment, meaning just the interest. When your payment just covers a little over the interest you will make those payments for years, while making no real impact on the balance and that becomes a steady income source for the bank. We cannot justify the need for consumer debt to buy something today that we will pay for months or years to come and pay a lot more than the price advertised.

If you are going to put something on credit and not pay in full, do not even look at the price tag because you will pay a lot more than the price you are looking at. If you feel you need to build your credit here's one way of doing it without risking to falling in the trap. Use it as if it was your bank account, transfer the money you are going to use before even spending the money this way you will not need to make a payment and it will already be covered. This way when you go buy something it is already paid for and you do not need to remember to pay for your bill.
.

SEVENTH STORY

There is no free lunch. Everything we want in our lives has a price. There is nothing really free and what we get free we do not see real value in it. When we pay for something we are more careful with it. I have noticed the bigger the price tag, the more care and value we give to that product. If you get something for one dollar you are not going to care about breaking it, and you will just replace it, without even thinking about it. It is the same thing for our goals the bigger they are, the higher the price we have to pay for them, which often is not money.

If you want to be an Olympic athlete, we all have an idea it takes years. During those years you need to train full time and give your best during every training session. Then you would need to compete on many levels before you even have a chance to represent your country. There is a reason many of us do not even consider this option, we know the price to pay is really expensive. When it comes to blood, sweat, and tears and you have no guarantee of ever winning a medal and when you do you want the gold but only a few of us can say we are the best in the world.

When you have big goals you know the price will be a lot but you have no idea how much it will be, all you can do is get started and never quit. If you get started, never quit and find a way to conquer every obstacle in your way, you will reach your final destination regardless of what others think. There was always someone who did it first. Some will say no one did it before, it cannot be done, while others will say, I will be the first one to do it. How we see things will enable us to get started or stop before we even get a chance to make the first move. Nothing comes to anyone without any prior effort, nothing of real value.

If something of value comes to us without effort, and even with effort, when it comes to money, it might just disappear and leave us standing there, wondering what happened? You need to be able to pay the price and that price is even harder when it comes to money. The reason is for some it is easy to make it, and for those who make it, they believe they will always be able to make more and do not even think about how they are managing what they have made. When you do not manage what you have made you will be left standing wondering what happened and even some of us seated on the sidelines are wondering what happened.

We are here looking at a great producer, someone who generated millions and see them broke and we are here thinking that would not be me. We have to remember they started from the bottom and got to the top without learning how to manage money and they were valuable enough to the marketplace to be worth that much in someone else eyes. One thing that did not change is their relationship with money. Yes they are making more but they have the same behavior they always had before, the only thing different is they can afford bigger items.

If we look at it this way, it is not about how much you make. How many millions that came your way but your ways of handling money. If your basic way of handling money is to spend more when I can afford more, you will find ways to spend it without even noticing it and this will happen at a faster rate and the money will be gone faster or at the same speed, you would have, if you were making less. When you have less to spend the items you are spending on are much smaller. When you have millions what you are spending is so much bigger you can spend millions in a month.

It does not take much time; there are some very expensive items we cannot even imagine thinking about from our point of view. The problem is, we look at someone who is broke after making millions or even hundreds of millions and we wonder how on earth did they do it? We cannot see it because we are seeing it using our view on life, which is made of items that are much less expensive. We look at cars that are less than 100k and we look at homes that are under one million for the majority of us. Then we wonder how they could spend so much that fast.

A lot of money is relative to the price of the items you are spending it on. When you have no limit or you think you have no limit financially, and you think that money will keep coming for years or even the rest of your life. The problem is we start with our old views and start spending on a different scale. We do not keep them at the same level. For the money to last, even if we are spending like crazy, it would be to stay at the same scale. The problem is when we change scale or lifestyle.

If you are making 50k a year and you buy items you can afford while being price conscious, you will get items that are not more than 1k when you are spending for fun. Your cellphone might not be over 1K. When you go shopping you will keep it under 1k. When you look for a home you will most likely keep it under 500k because you will consider that amount to be high and the time it will take you to pay the mortgage. If you go look for a car you will keep the cost of that car to something close to 50k or much less. Keeping that in mind you will be careful with your income and make sure you have something left.

The problem is if you go from that mindset and that price range to making millions, your lifestyle might change to look and be one of those millionaires. You might go shopping at stores where you can only leave spending a few thousands of dollars. You will get the best cellphone out there and replace it every 6months to a year and pay in full because you do not want any contract, after all, you can afford it now. You will buy the nicest home you can find and will not care about the price. You can now afford the best, meaning what is most expensive or even have your own home built.

When it comes to cars you will replace your car without even thinking about it. You will go for the top model, the high-end brand. You might even be one of the lucky few that gets to order a car that is not yet on the market and be one of the first to have it. After all, you do not want to see someone else driving the same car at every corner. You might want to be different from everyone else, after all, you are successful, and looking like everyone else might not be something you still want to do. After all, your life changed from 50k to millions.

Traveling will be something else too, the top suites and private resorts and diamonds hotels, only the best for you. No way will you want to be crammed in coach or economy with everyone else and their kids screaming and crying. You will go for first class only or travel on private planes, even own or rent yours. What was a limit or impossible before is now something that is open. When everything is open and you can pay for it in full, you do not even think about it's effects on you. When something is cheap in our eyes and we can afford it by just paying in full we do not see any warning signs.

For us, warning signs are only there when we have to choose the size of the payment. If we go deeper we see we cannot afford it here and now. What we doing is basically lowering the damages or the impact by choosing something we like within our price range and without getting in too much trouble. We think about it and go for it based on what we feel will not cause too much damage. We are conscious at some level that we are taking a risk and we have a limit of how much we are willing to risk for something we know is not that important but we still want.

Without warning signs, it is hard to know you are getting into trouble. If we could go to the dealership and pay cash for a brand new 100k car we would not see there is a problem there, after all, we can afford it, we are paying cash for it and we have millions. That is just 10% of a million what is the big deal. When you keep doing this and keep changing items based on a new one being nicer and being one of the first one to have it, you will lose a lot of money. You will not be able to sell what you bought for the price you got it for. That money will just be lost.

We are often expecting the best and always think only good things can come to us and the bad only happens to people we do not know, like people in other countries or the other side of town, but never really close to home and not to us. A very easy way to see this is how we spend money and the deals we take will are we think life will always be the same or improve. We rarely think things might go down and we might lose it all. We never see our lives like the stock market, with unpredictable ups and downs, with gains and losses. We think we are just going up and we will make more and reach higher and higher ground.

One way we do so without even realizing it is when we take out a loan or a mortgage. Let's say you take a car loan for 60 months and you calculate you can afford the payments. How did you calculate you could afford the payments? You did so by looking at how much you make and assuming you will make the same amount for the next 5 years. Is there any guarantee you will make that money for the next 5 years? You are predicting future income and attaching payment to that future income. You are spending money you have not even made yet.

Let say you also add a nice home to this because things are looking good. Again planning the future on past events, how long you have been working and how much you are making and the fact you will be making the same or more. Now you take out a mortgage for 25 years, that mortgage is a prediction. One that says I will make constantly enough to cover this amount, live and pay all my other bills for the next 25 years. To me, that is a gamble. No one can predict continuous employment for the next 25 years. Especially at the speed, everything is changing. There is no way you can know what will happen.

When you spend future income before you even made it you are taking risks. If you are no longer able to pay or cover the bills that item will be taken away and all the money you have paid will be gone and you will be left with nothing. This is the only reason why someone can lose it all and have nothing left and be homeless. When everything you have is paid for, no one can come and take it away because you cannot afford to pay for it anymore. If someone can come and take it away, it is not yours. If you are making payments to someone for an item, it is not yours.

What is yours, is what you have paid for in full. What you own outright is what is yours. Everything else you are using until it is paid for. People have this confused because they have been living somewhere for so long and the bank comes and takes it away because they can no longer afford the payments. It was not yours in the first place if it was yours the bank would not be able to take possession of it legally and have you evicted. If you are going to have payments, know that the item will be legally your one it is paid in full.

The owner of something is the one that has paid it in full. The bank paid it in full and you are reimbursing the bank. Many of us miss that simple fact. The bank purchased it outright and you have to pay back the bank with interest. You did not buy the house the bank bought it for you, using debt and putting your name on it. When you do not pay the bank they just take the asset back and sell it to someone else. That is the simplified way to explain what ownership is so you can have a clear picture.

When you do this on a car that will never increase the value you are doing a bad deal regardless of your interest rate and terms of payments. Once again the lender bought this item at the listed price in full and he is basically reselling it to you with interest. You are buying what looks like the same car but you are paying more for it because you had someone else get it for you because you could not afford to pay cash for it. When you have a lot of cash you pay the price tag. Everyone else just pays the price tag with interest.

The price we have to pay in our society is patience, we need to have the patience to save and manage our money. We have seen time and time again that money is not the answer but we have missed it. The lottery winner's who goes back to being broke is normal when you think about it. If the only thing you did in your life is spend everything you had when you have more you will do what you have been doing all your life, which is spend everything you have. It should not be a surprise that the money did not solve their problems.

When your problem is spending, more money will allow you to spend even more. This is why some of those same lottery winners have bigger problems now than they had before. They spend more than they had and used credit now that the money is gone they cannot afford the payments for the items they are using. If you do not find a way to manage what you have more money will not help you in any way it will allow you to do more of the same. When you do more of the same it can be good or bad depending on the actions you are taking.

Poor money management does not care about how much you are making. Regardless of how much you are making it will be all gone. When you have no plans and all you do is buy what you want, how can you have anything left? You did not plan to have anything left. In order to have money aside, you need to put money aside, without the habit of setting money aside, all your money will just be gone and remembering how you spend it will be hard if not impossible. The funny thing with money is, if you do not plan to save and invest you will have nothing left, money loves to be managed.

Anyone that has money set aside had to plan for it and do it. It did not just happen because they wanted it to. Actions must be taken and constant action too, because it is something you need to do more than once. But the good thing is, you can have it on autopilot. What you see you will spend if you are not disciplined and not strong enough to resist clever marketing and the latest new products. Having this money away from the main bank account you are using is the way to go if you wish to have something left.

The price to pay in the society we are living in is the ability to decide what is best for us and to do it. It involves the ability to say no and resist buying every new product that will be replaced within months or less than a year. You can set up your own time frame to upgrade your items, it does not have to be every time there is a new product, you change and pay for it and get into debt to afford it. You can decide you will change for example your cellphone, every two years this way you have time to save for a new one and the amount will be fine with you because you know it was something planned and not just something you bought just because the manufacturer launched a new one.

You have to be able to handle not having the latest of everything that comes out. This will allow you to be in a different place than the majority of people. When you are able to delay the gratification of getting an item when it comes out, on credit or taking a loan, you will be free and you will own what you buy without paying more for it. You cannot look for a deal, negotiate the price and get a loan for it. You will be paying more for it in the end. We often miss this simple fact.

If you want something there is a price to pay and for that price to have no interest when it comes to objects, you will need to pay for it in full at the store the moment you buy it. We live in a culture of 'let me get this now and pay for it as I am using it.' When you do this, you are assuming you will always be able to afford it. If anything changes, your ability to afford it changes. When it comes to paying something cash you know you can afford it today and you do not need to think about the ability to afford it later.

When it comes to our finances the price to pay for freedom, meaning not having payments for our consumer goods is to pay cash for it all. In order to be able to pay anything cash, we need to be able to be disciplined and save for it. The ability to save and plan will allow us to get what we want without bringing home a payment. For this, to work we need to spend less than we make and save the rest. To spend less than you make you have to use only the income you are making and not use credit and pay it after, while you are spending the money you were going to put on the card and will have to wait for your next paycheck.

Since we know more money will not help anyone who is in the habit of spending it all. We have to learn to start saving a portion of what we make and when we make more we have to save a portion of that income. Saving needs to increase with income not just spending. If we only increase spending and lifestyle when we make more, will we not have anything to show for it or than objects that have no value and have been replaced by new models. The first step will be to put aside a small percentage like 1% of your take-home pay.

Do it for a month a see how it feels. Next month increase it to 2% and keep doing this until it becomes easy for you and there are no limits. It will help you with your spending because you will have to be more conscious because you have less to spend. When we live on 100% of our income if anything happens, we are out in the streets since we have nothing to replace our income. You will need to practice doing this to have at least one month of your pay set aside, this way you have a month of everything covered but keep going. Your next goal should be for whatever is important to you, but lowering your payments should also be a goal to keep in mind.

If you have no debt and you pay your car faster, you will then be able to save for many months of peace of mind. The price for peace of mind is to have enough saved that even if your job is gone you keep everything you have. It can happen to anyone at any time but when you prepare for the worst while still expecting the best you will be fine regardless of what happens. Knowing that if your job is gone you will be fine for a few months or a year is enough to be excited about and you only have to do it once..

THEN THERE WAS THE END

Life is not what we expect it to be. Life happens in a way we cannot even begin to think how it will happen and where it will lead. This was the way this book was written in a way anything goes. Writing what comes to mind with a basic idea where I thought it was going but in the end, it became something totally different. This was just my introduction to you; there will be a lot more to come. This was not written to please you or get your approval.

This was written in a way for you to think and see things differently, other than you have to be programmed to see them. Yes, we have all been programmed with preconceived ideas of how things are and my goal with this introduction was to shock you enough to think about things differently. For you to start seeking your own meaning for things, instead of just taking anyone else's. That of course, also means mine as well. If you have noticed, I do not give you any answers but leave you with questions and ask you questions.

I do try to leave you with a way to get started that is somewhat the opposite of what you have been doing. Since I do not know you and your story, there are a lot of generalizations here that may not be you or the way you see and act. Those are there to have you see one of the most common sides of society. The one that is promoted to us, the one that is advertised and the one most of us are used to seeing when we look around or when we turn on the television.

There was too much to cover here and this would have been too long. So the initial goal was to get you started, get you thinking and most importantly have you see there are many ways of seeing things and not one way of doing things and you are able to do anything you wish to do if you have the courage to start and persevere. Life is what you make of it, not the cards you were dealt with when you got here. Everything happens to all of us, where you end up is more a question of how you steered your life.

You can start with a nice hand to play with and play the wrong cards at the wrong time and lose it all. You can start with a bad hand of and play your cards at the right time and end up where you did not believe you will end up, and where no one else expected you to end up. The opinions of others do not have to be your reality that is up to you to choose. When you let others decide what is true for you, you then limit your ultimate destination.

In life you will need mentors, someone that is ahead of you, someone that will believe in you, someone that will push you where you said you want to go and most importantly someone that will be who you need, not what you want. Someone that can be hard on you when you are too soft, someone that will be loving and caring when you are down and lend you a hand to help you get back up. I have had times I needed mentors and I did find them in books and audiotapes I would watch and listen to over and over until that moment passed.

Seek mentors; seek someone wiser, someone who has a different view of the world and someone who will be there to help you reach what you want to reach. Someone that is action oriented that will lead you to act. Someone that will be there, not always when you need it, but when you are ready. You might say you want one and you need one today, but this can only be determined with your actions and openness to set aside everything you think you know, so you can learn something new.

This is why there is always the saying you have to come with an empty cup. You have to do things you think will not and do not matter. In essence, you just have to follow and at some point, you will see where you were going. Just like those old Karate Kid movies where Daniel thinks he is wasting his time and Mr. Miagi finally shows him what he has been learning. He then got the understanding and was ready to do the work. There is also the saying: The teacher appears when the student is ready.

What I have seen in my life is, the teacher is known when you start thinking about it, when you are ready you can go to him. What I mean by this is even if Daniel in the original Karate kid movies was doing all this work and spending all this time he was not fully ready. He was focused on what he thought he needed and what ways he thought he would be doing them. He was really invested when he saw results, meaning when he saw how this could be applied, that is the reason he did not quit when he was about to walk away.

In life, when life itself is your mentor, you cannot scream at it and ask it "show me what all this was for? I wanted to have this and this is the life I am leading, you are not helping me at all." While in fact you were being trained. We are always nearsighted and do not see the full picture when someone who is your mentor is training you, remember you will not fully see or understand where they are leading you. So you need to find someone you trust and someone who cares more about helping you achieve your own goals then what they have to teach you or them being involved.

A great mentor will let you know they are not the one for you and that you will need to find someone else. You both have to choose each other, you cannot just ask someone to be your mentor and expect them to just agree. They have to see the raw material in you, that desire inside to do whatever it takes to succeed. Not the ability to say whatever it takes. The ability to talk a good game and the skills to play a good one are totally different. This has nothing to do with your past or who you are, but if you are ready. Let's remember that the Karate Kid movie was a movie.

In life, your mentor might not be as nice but the goal is not to be nice, but to push you enough so you do what needs to be done. Sometimes we are totally clueless about what needs to be done and how to do it. This is a good time for you not to share anything you think you already know because if you knew it and knew where to get started you could do it and would have done it. Real mentors are busy, they have their own lives and their interactions with you might be short, but it does not need to be long, short and effective is the way your mentor should be.

One thing I have noticed is everyone wise, wants a mentor but very few know how to be a protégé. They fake it until they cannot take it anymore and lash out. They stay and take enough of what the mentor told them and become the competition and believe they are better than the mentor, one thing they do not know is the mentor never reveals it all and the mentor is always ahead, that is a truly wise one. So there is nothing you can steal that can make you better, yes you can start your own thing and copy what he taught you, but you do not have what he has.

You know the motions but cannot explain why. You are doing what he taught you but he only taught you in this way because of who you are, while he will teach someone else in a totally different way. He will always adapt his teaching to the student in front of him. How can you be like, or even think you can copy or be better than your mentor? When you understand what you saw and the way you were taught was only because of who you are and not necessarily the way to do it for everyone. That is when you will know your only goal is to be the best you can be.

You can learn to play a sport from a professional athlete, but you will not be able to start a coaching company and do what he does. Because there is so much more than what he taught you, that has to do with who you are, how your body is and how to reach your highest potential. A mentor is someone who looks at you and finds the best way to help you achieve your true potential. It is not a one fit all approach. There might be some general basic ideas he wants people to learn, but there will be a point where true changes happen, and that is when it is one on one.

In order to be a protégé you need to accept and mostly understand this, that what you are seeing is for you and for you only. You need to be someone honest enough that your main goal is not to get close to someone, learn from them, then turn around and try to do the same thing. We are all here to do different things so there is no need to try to be like anyone else. When you do this, you make life much harder and you always have to copy, you cannot innovate because that is not who you are and what you are meant to do.

You can only create and innovate when you are doing what you are here to do or when you are doing what you love to do and not what makes money. You need to have your own passion and where you want to go. We are so used to work for money and have been taught to do what works, that we often missed the life lesson of being who we are. Be who you are, do not try to be what works for someone else because you will always be waiting for them to come up with something new to copy it. We have all noticed this in the marketplace; the leader creates, while followers copy.

Your goal in life should not be to be like anyone else but to be you. Be the best you that you can be, no one can beat you at being you. When you try to be someone else, they will always beat you because they are themselves. You also have to understand that your mentor might not want what you want and might have a different definition of success. For some people their definition of success is to have a lot of followers, people they tell what to do, while for others it is to create leaders who can do things on their own and do not need them. One makes it about them the other makes it about you.

Your mentor might not be that far on his journey yet, but you will be able to tell by the way he talks, the way he sees the world and how he expresses' himself or herself. You can see that this person is different and at one point everything will be different for them. You cannot always look for physical clues once again they do not want what everyone wants and do not show it in ways everyone does. They have a different view of life and what they want out of life. You knowing who they are and how much they have is not important to them.

They are more concerned about everyone feeling good and at ease around them, then showing off what they have or what they can do. They are more interested in you then talking about themselves or what they are doing or what they have done. You will have a hard time having them share things about themselves, not because they have anything to hide, but because the goal is to help you and you learning everything about them does not tell you anything about you. They are not celebrity minded, desiring of being in the limelight.

I am talking here about a true mentor that is in the world, but not of it. That lives on this planet but is not like anyone else you ever met, someone you cannot guess what they are thinking, even if you are watching the same thing. Someone that needs to explain things in a way you will understand not because he is superior but because his view of the world is totally different from the one you have seen. Someone who expresses his uniqueness and does not apologize for it and does not try to be like everyone else.

Someone who acts the same way in public as well as when they are alone. Someone who has nothing to hide and who is truly honest in every setting. If you have the chance to meet someone like this, the best thing you can do is listen and ask when he or she is done talking, ask questions on how to reach your own goals, because, in the end, we want to know what we can take from this and how this can help us. Remember he or she will not do anything for you but will only help you get started, helping you stay motivated and have you think differently. The role of a mentor is to help you achieve your full potential not do it for you.

This being said, I would like to thank you for taking the time to read this. Remember I did not do this for me but for you, if it helped you, great. If it did not, then go out there and keep reading until you find someone that does. The goal is to never stop learning and keep growing in the direction of where you want to go. This was not about me, but about you. In helping you, I hope to see a different world and how everything is. If it was not different levels, there would only be one class or one level we would all be in it.

What you have and who you are is based on your personal choices and decisions. But for this to be true you have to make your own choices and think for yourself and not just agree with anyone, yes I included. Do not agree with me or disagree with me, but take the time to look at what I have presented here and see if it can help you if you applied it and where it could lead you if you thought that way. When you agree or disagree, all you do is set the knowledge aside and continue what you were doing.

The goal of this introduction was to get you started. Giving you hope that nothing is over until you quit and even if you have quit in the past it is never too late to get back in the game. It will only be too late when you are dead. Until then it is up to you to decide what you want out of life, learn enough about it that you have an idea where to get started and keep going until you reach it. One thing that is often forgotten is before you do, you must be and to be you need to work enough on yourself to have the mindset of someone who achieves their dreams.

I am sure you have noticed that most people give up on their dreams and have been told by others who have given up to do the same. How funny is that? That someone who has given up is telling you to give up? Are you sure that is the type of person you want to get advice from when it comes to your dreams? If you want to do something, learn from someone who has done it and learn what it takes, whom you have to be what you need to be doing and then do it your way. But you do need to have some basic qualities and attitudes about life if you want to be happy and living the dream life awake.

Successful people have things in common regardless of what they have achieved. You will want to study those successful people and read a book about them and what made them successful from a human being perspective. You want to follow leaders; people who are living and doing things most do not dare dream of doing. You will see, they will tell you to keep your dream alive, the will tell you not to quit, those are the ones you need to ask about living a different life. People, in general, will tell you what they know based on the life they are living.

If you want to be a business owner, do not ask employees what they think about it. For them, it might be a nightmare and too much work and not even worth to get started. While if you ask a business owner he might tell you that is a lot of work but it does not feel like work because they love it. When you love what you do, you do not see it as work and you have a good time and cannot wait to get back at it. You need to ask people who are doing what you want to do, do not ask someone that does not have the same goals, otherwise, they might not encourage you to even pursue it.

You might say, "I do not know anyone, I live in a small town, I live in a poor country how I do this?" Do it like most of us do, read books, listen to audio books and go to seminars. Now you can order ebooks online get them right away and you do not even need to wait for them in the mail. You are your best friend or your worst enemy. You are the one that will stop you, no one else. For anyone else to stop you, you have to give them the power to do so and to agree with them. This is your life, live it the way you want to live it and the people that stay in your life are the ones that were meant to be there in the first place.

Dare to be who you are, dare to live your dreams. You can also be mentored by people that are no longer here and who have left what they know and what helped them in a book. Learn from great people who were the movers of the past. Learn from the movers and shakers of the present. But make sure you learn, otherwise, you will continue what you have been doing and not much will change. If you want your life to change you need to change. Because anyone that has things you do not have is doing things differently. Some have written books on how to do it, follow their recipe but add your own twist to it once you have succeeded.

In the beginning, follow someone else's recipe and do not change it because if you already knew how to do it, you would have. Admit you do not know and listen to someone else. Once you have reached your goals then add your own spin to it but do not try to improve when you get started. Once you have reached a level of success then try your own way and see where it goes. If it fails, it does not matter you are already successful and if it succeeds, then great, you are even more successful. Use this win-win formula before you start thinking you know.

It was a pleasure for me to write those few words. If you wish to know more about me and how I can help you with the mindset and what you need to succeed in anything you wish to do, then get in touch with me and we can go from there. If not, take time to reflect, read this again and find a way to get started, I wish you the best.

You can reach me at www.masteryourpersonalfinance.com

www.ingramcontent.com/pod-product-compliance
Lightning Source LLC
Chambersburg PA
CBHW020603220526
45463CB00006B/2430